DISCOVERED ROADS

JAMIE INGLIS

PROHIBITED PUBLICATIONS
MMXIX

Discovered Roads
© Jamie Inglis 2019.
Paperback First Edition B&W
ISBN 978 1 9995975 3-5

The right of Jamie Inglis to be identified as the author of this work has been asserted by him in accordance with the Copyright, Designs and Patents Act, 1998. All rights reserved. No part of this publication may be reproduced without the express consent of the author.

The cover is *Padrão dos Descobrimentos, Monument to the Discoverers,* on the North Bank of the Targus River at Belem near Lisbon.
It celebrates the Portuguese Age of Discovery in the 15th and 16th Century.
The figure at the apex is Henry the Navigator.

Satellite images p3, and from 9/12 p49 © Google.
Burning dollars p17 © Shutterstock, Lightning p18 © Mircea Madau
White smoke at the Vatican p20 © Vatican TV.
Air Traffic images p30 © flightradar24.com, and © ADSB.
Mona Lisa p32 © RMN Grand Palais (Louvre)/Michel Urtado.
Frontline image p41 © Prisma/Jamie Inglis, Repatriation p46 © PA
CCTV images p60 © Shutterstock, Network Images p90 © pixabay.com
6th Battalion QOCH at Loos by Joseph Gray p99 © The Highlanders' Museum
Breaking News images p102/3 © CNN and others.
All photographs and other images © Jamie Inglis 2019.

New Neologisms - new words for new times.   newneologisms.com
The Disorganised Society - real life is disorganised.   disorganised.org
The Science Fiction Index – the best of all time.   sci-fi-index.com
Burning the Page - from Paper to Pixel.   burningthepage.com

Created with Lulu

PROHIBITED PUBLICATIONS   prohibitedpublications.com
79 Bruntsfield Place
Edinburgh
EH1O 4HG
Scotland

ISBN 978-1-9995975-3-5

also by jamie inglis

 *the geometer's dreams (1992)*

 *fractals & mnemonics (1996)*

 *hold on (2000)*

 *collected poems 1985 – 1999 (2009)*

 *gluon notes (2006)*

 *experience engines (2010)*

Warning

Do **not** stop now
Do **not** look up
Do **not** listen further

Do **not** speak
Do **not** ask
Do **not** question

Do **not** see
Do **not** imagine
Do **not** understand

Do **not** think
Do **not** wonder
Do **not** refuse

Do **not** turn
Do **not** worry
Do **not** change

Do **not** stand
Do **not** act
Do **not** move

Do **not** do this
Do **not** do that
Do **not** now stop

Do **not** do anything
Do **not** do now
Do **not** do nothing

Discovered Roads

Previously – *Experience Engines*
The Pointless Club   2   Touching the Fire Dragon   3
Mr CIA Man on the ferry to New Amsterdam   4
The last war we fought on our own   7
The Beach at Waikiki   8   A Minute to Midnight   9

First Roads
Start Here/Intro   11   Commuter Journey   12
First Steps   13   Mothers still waiting   15
The Bonfire of the Banks   16   Fred the Shed   17
Lightning on the Links   18   On the Train Again   19
A Strong God Delusion Moment   21

Travelled Roads
Masters of Time   23   Mesmerised by dreams   24
Cars Need Fuel   25   Dreams of Barak   26
Later   27   Continuous Friends / A Set of Lines   28
The end of New Labour   29   Forty-eight hours of no fly   31
Mona Lisa [The Celebrity]   33   The iterations of the day   34
Starting off in the wrong direction   35
A million photos of Pompeii   37   Decluttering   38
Back-stories   39   In the Eye   40

from a frontline living room
Iraq plus five   42   02.19AM GMT 20/03/08   43
Oradour-sur-Glane   45   Bringing all the bodies home   46
Walking   47   Ten years on   49   Trident   50

Social Media Cul-de-sacs
Poem for Facebook™   52   Poem for Facebook™ V2.0   53
Twitter™ Poem   55   Twitter™ Poem 2   56
Twitter™ Poem 2A   56

Social Media Cul-de-sacs cont.
Twitter™ Poem 3   57   Twitter™ Poem 3B   58
Poem for Search Engines™   59   Last Seen on CCTV   60
Never Alone   61   Catching-up   62
Immersed in a Virtual Environment   63   Engrained   64

The Road back to Verdun
Verdun and The Somme   67   Verdun Now   68
Sur le TGV Again   69   First Night Verdun   71
Walking through the woods   73   Verdun Woods 2   75
Men and Mud   76   At the Ossuaire   77
Between their time and the future   79
Le Tranchee des Baionnettes   81
A Centenary approaches   83   They shall not pass   85

Fourth Stage Navigation
AR: Augmented Reality   89   The Armies of Memory   90
Backing-Up   91   A Darwinian Dead End   92
Haunted by Malthus   92   Tidemarks   93
Out of time   93   Looking for Zen Thrills   95
A New Dragon Year   96   Saving this Spot   97
The End of the Olympics   98   The Good Old Days   99
Order and Disorder   100   Distractions   101
Tomorrow's news cycle   103
Among the commuters on the train   104
Rubbish Seagulls   105   Virtual Life Lag   106

more New Neologisms
A net to catch the web   109
TimeJolt   110   MindedTo   110   textexit   111
TimeDart   111   ChaosFix   112   FlatMeme   112
ZeroDees   113   EmitTime   113   digitock   114
SoWhatSo   114   DoNoInfo   115

fragments and colophons
Going to Gozo   116
End of the day poem of the leftover words   120

Previously

The Pointless Club

All the streets are numbered there,
somewhere between heaven and here.
Long passageways full of secret keys.
A lost island locked in the trees.

All the avenues are numbered there,
some oasis that we all share.
Beyond the maze that is despair,
life's utopia for all to compare.

All the roads are numbered there,
somewhere between heaven and here.
Many crossroads full of hidden signs,
our island, always our times.

Touching the Fire Dragon

Perched on the caldera's rim.
A rumble builds beneath your feet
and blows the explosion through your soles.
Add deafening sound and the caldera erupts.
Throwing tons of lava and rocks towards the clouds.
A molten vertical river rising before your eyes
and turning and raining back down below your feet.
A searing red retinal streak.
Touched, the Fire Dragon.

Mount Yasur, Tanna Island, Vanuatu (2005)

Mr CIA Man on the ferry to New Amsterdam

New Amsterdam ferry with Mr CIA.
A lie from the first about crossing from Suriname.

Investigating murders in these here parts.
Superintendent killed was it that?
New York City cop now working for Justice.
A reconnaissance of possible hostile.
We're on holiday no knowledge of murders.
From Scotland, not Irish and IRA.

The ferry started loading, Mr CIA to his armour.
Only gates were opening still time to wonder.
No cars were moving yet Mr CIA.
Only people from everywhere crossing over today.

Mr CIA doesn't know the length of the crossing.
I speak politely to people passing. Thirty minutes.
Going back to speak to Mr CIA alarms the spooks.
Set Mr CIA on edge for thirty entertaining minutes.

An unknown quantity relaxing and smoking on the ferry to New Amsterdam with Mr CIA.
With armoured 4x4, partner and locals.

Still not Irish, no thanks to a Guinness.
Water on the ferry to New Amsterdam,
                         courtesy of Mr CIA.
Happy to banter with locals, joking and in your face.

Wary of inconsistencies is the unknown stranger.
Watching Mr CIA wonder,
on the ferry to New Amsterdam.

Las Malvinas War Memorial, Buenos Aires (2008)

Argentinian 50 Peso note introduced 2015

The last war we fought on our own

Twenty-five years after Gotcha
modest remembrance of the end of empire.
One thousand deaths in a short war
for our Falkland Overseas Territories.

Twenty-five years after the Belgrano,
Sheffield, Sir Galahad, Atlantic Conveyer and more.
To watery graves in the South Atlantic
and barren hillside graves, in the South Atlantic.

Twenty-five years after hostilities
only we and Argentina remember.
Would we act the same today
for our Falkland Overseas Territories?

April 2007

The Beach at Waikiki

Walking the beach at Waikiki.
Diamond Head brooding at our back.
Browning bodies bake prone on the sand
waves roll through thousands in the sea.
Foaming at the waterline, a scum of factor
reflecting oil slicks on the surface of the sea.

Through a sinking sunset watched
mostly by silent American and Japanese eyes
from countless cocktail bars and grills.
The towering concrete of rooms and suites behind
encasing the dream of the beach at Waikiki.

A Minute to Midnight 19.03.03

A minute to midnight
to invade Iraq.

A minute to midnight
how will they fight back.

A minute to midnight
why do we attack?

A minute to midnight
Invasion Iraq.

A minute to midnight
not too late to turn back.

A minute to midnight
and the start of the flack.

A minute to midnight
standby Iraq.

A minute to midnight
Goodbye Iraq.

First Roads

Start Here / Intro

First starting to look.
No, I mean really look.
What can you see?
A few lines in front of you.
Stop, look around
what you really see
is all around you.
Just take the time to look.

Commuter Journey

Commuter journey
Again and again
Exact same stations
Again and again
There and back
Again and again
Routines establishing
Again and again
Time has passed
Again and again
Where did it go?
Again and again.

Poetry on the train
Again and again.

First Steps

The first step a sense of direction
an outline appears of the route.
Direction and meaning flood the senses
new imperatives force themselves forward.

Second steps often self-selecting
and detail appears of some of the route.
Uncertainty and ignorance challenge the decisions
the companions shepherding
      to the next bit of wisdom.

Mothers of the Disappeared outside the Presidential Palace, Buenos Aires (2008)

Mothers still waiting

Mothers still waiting
After years have passed
Still waiting
After decades have passed

Mothers still waiting
For sons and daughters
Still waiting
For sisters and brothers

Mothers still waiting
Circling the square
Still waiting
With photos of the disappeared

Mothers still waiting
In hope not fear
Still waiting
For answers to appear

Mothers still waiting
Fewer every year
Still waiting
For the truth to be clear

The Bonfire of the Banks

Great economic days
Great economic daze

Banks are reeling
Depositors are running
Shareholders are ruined

Banks are nationalised
Depositors are numb
Shareholders are still ruined

Banks are ours
Everyone loses but bankers
Taxpayers pick up the bill

Great economic haze
Great economic maze

08.10.08
Banks nationalised

Fred the Shed

Sir Fred the Shed
where are you now?
Our lives in shreds
come take a bow.

Sir Fred the Shed
no doubt in hiding now.
Our lives in debt,
to you we kowtow?

Sir Fred the Shed
the banker run out of town.
Our lives spent repaying
the wankers
who turned out to be clowns.

Lightning on the Links

Deeper quiet after the storm
Lightning strikes then silence
Wave fronts passing outwards
Sonic cloud of mighty decibels
Structures shake at the storms heart
One moment, the storm has passed
Deeper silence after the storm

But the moment has not passed
A further flash of light
Crash then silence supersound

Lightning over Oradea, Romania © Mircea Madau

On the Train Again

On the train, yet again
looking for lines, that old refrain.

On the train, time and again
looking for a start, a point to regain.

On the train, forever again
looking for a voice, speaking plain.

On the train, always ends again
looking for a mark, to ease the pain.

© Vatican TV

© Vatican TV

A Strong God Delusion Moment

The crescendo of The God Delusion
when a hundred elderly male cardinals
are cloistered for the Papal conclave.

The apex of The God Delusion
when no-one applies to be Pope
and God tells the others how to vote.

The fanfare of The God Delusion
when artificial white smoke appears
and a new Peter waves to the crowds.

Travelled Roads

Jesuitic Mission of *Santisima Trinidad del Parana*,
Encarnation, Paraguay

Masters of Time

Masters of this moment
and the last one.
Masters of this moment
and the next one.

Masters of every moment
and of each one.
Masters of the first moment
and the last one.

Masters of our moment
and every other one.
Masters of your moment
and those to come.

Mesmerised by dreams

Mesmerised by the dreams that never materialised.
Waking to the dawn of what is real life.
Visions of a future devoid of the truth.
Memories now of what should have been.

Innocence lost with the intervals of time.
Fading aspirations with the failure of inspiration.
Evaporating hope of the heights of desire.
Memories now of what should have been.

Mesmerised by the dream that materialised.
Reminded always, that reality is man-made.
Singular choices shaping what lies ahead.
Memories now of what has been.

Cars Need Fuel

A lifetime watching the fuel gauge
Every cycle starting at full
Every drive reducing it further
Till the fuel gauge reaches the red zone
Then the fuel gauge is returned to full.

Repeat, Repeat, Repeat.
Repeat, Repeat, Repeat.
Repeat, Repeat, Repeat.

A lifetime of repeating the cycle
Cars need fuel
To get you from A to B
The price you pay
Goes up every day.

Dreams of Barak

A new face at the top of the table
promising change from the old world order.

A new hope at the dawn of depression
promising bailouts for everything bust.

A new vision for a new century
promising consensus as the only way ahead.

A new man we never thought we'd see
promising to be different for all the world to see.

A new man at the top of the world
promising all things are possible.

Later

Later, after the moment had passed
A voice whispered sweetly in my ear
Notions of distant memory and loss
Awakening a primitive, older fear.

Longer, after the moment has passed by
The voice growing fainter but still near
Suggests a forgotten time and moment
Illuminating a modern, timeless here.

**Continuous Friends /
 A Set of Lines**

Paths crossing again.　　　Paths crossing again.
Another moment　　　　　Another moment
we meet again.　　　　　　we meet again.

Paths cross again.
Continuous moments
as we meet again.

Paths recrossing again.
More moments
spent together again.

Paths crisscrossing again.
Fleeting moments
as we pass again.

Paths crossout again.
Missed moments
lost to us again.

Paths crossover again.
Discontinuous moments
till we meet again.

The end of New Labour 11.05.10

The era of New Labour ends today.
A statesman from Fife leaves with his children
and the new child from the old Tories,
with pregnant wife walks into the glare.

Thirteen years of New Labour ends today.
A new political landscape starts this day
and the new child of coalition(s)
will be the offspring of every future election day.

Flight Radar image 16.04.10

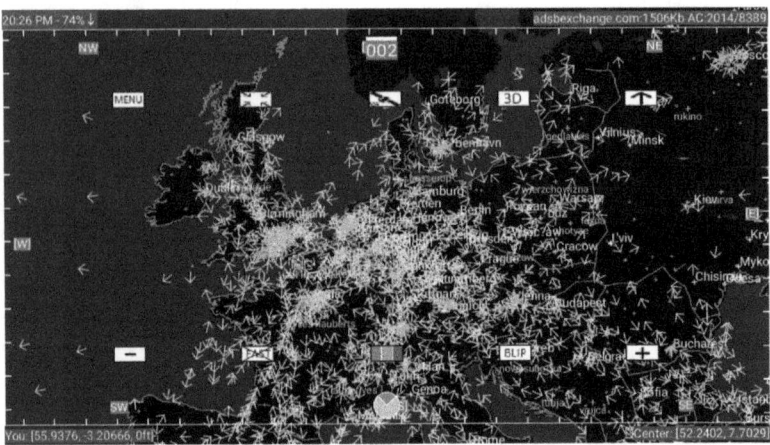
ADSB Air Traffic image, June 2018

Forty-eight hours of no fly

Not a cloud or a contrail to be seen,
the skies over Scotland
the bluest they've ever been.
Severe clear the pilots call it.

A volcano in Iceland clears the sky
not a single vapour trail up on high.
No movement through the sky,
only birds flying not very high
through a deserted azure sky.
Thanks to Iceland's dust up high
before our eyes a truly unique sky.

Northern Europe
No fly zone 15 - 23 April 2010

Mona Lisa Reality

Mona Lisa Virtual
© RMN-Grand Palais (musée du Louvre) / Michel Urtado

Mona Lisa   [The Celebrity]

The world's first celebrity painting
surrounded by crowds snapping away.
I must warn you the next experience
always contains flash photography.

The world's first stationary celebrity.
Flickering constantly
behind a barrage of flashguns.
Crowds surrounding, swirling, closing-in
flashing, then moving away.
Every day the same experience
ten thousand digital images more.

The world's first unknown celebrity.
Countless strangers
stopping for a few moments.
Press the button
record the scene,
miss the experience.
That knowing smile,
suits us even more now.

The iterations of the day

The iterations of the day
The routines of our life
That we measure every day
And chart the passing of our life.

The iterations of the day
The subroutines we dance
So many times every day
And mark our passing in a trance.

The iterations of the day
The cycles turned another way
Each one different every day
Leaving a mark, who can say.

Starting off in the wrong direction

Turning north away from the sun
and the mirrors of mortal vanity.
Bright lures of fascinating snares
corroding the hearts of those less wary.

Turning north away from the sun
footsteps avoiding the beaten path
and the baubles of broken mortality
corrupting the brains of those less wary.

Turning north away from the sun
into the darkness of increasing uncertainty
for fresh light beyond the decay
capturing the minds of those still wary.

Pompeii

A million photos of Pompeii

How many photos of Pompeii
are taken every day?

Twenty thousand visitors
on a busy day at Pompeii.

With digital cameras and phones
pointing every which way.

How many photos each of Pompeii
do they take in their one day?

At least fifty photos each
during their visit to Pompeii.

And a million 'new' photos of Pompeii
taken every single day, including today.

Decluttering

Lightening loads all and each of us carry.

Shelves, drawers, cupboards, cellars.
Yielding detritus, hoarding, memories and more.
Collected, accumulated, saved and hidden.

Everything taking up space and time.
Removing frees the space and mind,
to move on less weighted down.

Back-stories

Creating back-stories
in the photos of strangers.
Two people hidden from recognition
hands in front of faces.
Spotted in the later, and larger review.
Prompting the stranger
to create a back-story
for the two people
possibly hiding? from recognition.

In the Eye

Standing in the eye of the hurricane
Standing in the eye of a monster storm
After the wind has done half its worst
The landscape flattened all around
Sudden Silence
The other side of the hurricane
The other side of the monster
Still to come
Silence stretches on

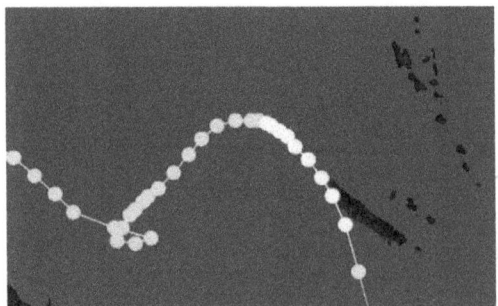

Severe Tropical Storm Freda (March 1982)

from a frontline living room

Iraq plus five

No end in sight
No sight of the end.

No sign of light
Around the next bend.

Five years of US might
A Hegemony to defend.

Neutrals taking flight
No-one left to tend.

Bombings a daily sight
(and) funerals to attend.

Soldiers patrol the night
Civilians left to fend.

Baghdad a building site
No-one left to mend.

No end in sight
No sight of the end.

23.01.08
Iraq War 5 years on
DoD – 'no end in sight'

02.19AM GMT 20/03/08

Five years after Shock and Awe
the US inhabits a wound still raw.

Five years after the invasion of Iraq
everyone's still waiting for the soldiers
                                to come back.

Five years after the terrorists arrived
more fear and terror and deaths
                              have been contrived.

Five years after the dictator was deposed
no WMD or terror links have been exposed.

Five years after the casualties started
no-one knows how many have departed.

Five years into an illegal war
strong hearts needed to heal the scar.

Five years in and no end in sight
whoever thought this was right?

                                                20.03.08
                            5th anniversary Iraq invasion
9.19PM 19/03 US, 2.19AM 20/03 UK, 5.19AM 20/03 Baghdad

Oradour-sur-Glane, France (2009)

Oradour-sur-Glane
10th June 1944

Sunny Saturday afternoon.
A modern circle of iron seals the city.
Only entry through the Centre Memoire
past an exhibition to another massacre.

Silence in the City Martyre
for 642 people silenced in a day.
Blackened, shells of buildings line the street.
Dr. Jacques Desourteaux's burnt out car
the only object still on the street.

A church, without worshippers.
Full of murmuring respectful voices
eyes turning up to the open sky above.

An hour passes and the town becomes history.
Only a memory of the massacre remains today.
Respect and remembrance
the purpose of the day.

Bringing all the bodies home

Now we bring all our soldiers home
No more corner of a foreign field
Planted forever with fallen military men.

All the coffins come home
One or more at a time
Through a silent parade
To their home town.

Now we bring all the bodies home
No more hidden in foreign fields
Every death seen
one too many.

© PA

Walking

Walking in waking minefields
Stumbling through subliminal shields
Testing each treacherous footstep
Searching for seekers also in step

A friend from before we became sane
Both mad inside the institution
Both mad outside the institution
When we could pretend we were sane

Twin Towers 9/12

Pentagon 9/12

Ten years on

The wars in Afghanistan and Iraq
are still going on
but only two more years
until we move on.

Still soldiers on the frontline
wherever that is.
And now we have Syria
to add to the (our) list.

The War on Terror, which left long ago
is now against the Jihadists
and all of their friends
and they have the time.

After a failed foreign adventure
all we leave behind
are the markers for those
with no more time.

Trident

A nuclear relic from the cold war
that no-one needs any more.

A weapon of last and first resort
to fire back after or before
the nuclear holocaust that is no more.

Bombs come in backpacks and briefcases now
and individual soldiers who know they will die.

Our new Ironclads are pie in the sky.
A last resort relic to throw overboard.

Social Media cul-de-sacs

Rembrandt's *The Night Watch*
The Reichsmuseum, Amsterdam

Poem for Facebook™
[no time for poetry]

Everyone is too busy for poetry these days,
hours online on Facebook™ accounts.

What are you doing today, tomorrow, next day?
Spending hours on Facebook™ mounts.

No time for poetry in networked days,
updating Facebook™ is all that counts.

Poem for Facebook™ V2.0
[no time for poetry]

Everyone is busy writing these days.
Hours online on Facebook™ accounts.

What you are doing and thinking every day.
Hours spent on Facebook™ inexorably mounts.

New time for poetry in networked days,
but updating Facebook™ is not what counts.

Try not to poke me after I'm gone.
23.02.10

The Night Watch 3D
Rembrandtplein (Rembrandt Square) **Amsterdam**

Twitter™ Poem

Look at what I'm doing now   26
                                                1

Look what I'm doing now   23
                                                1

Look what I'm doing now   23
                                                1

Look what I'm doing now   23
                                               98
                                                1

Look what I'm doing now   23
                                               122
                                                1

Look what I'm doin
                                                140

Shake that shiny hand,   *get in the picture*

Twitter™ Poem 2

Look at what I'm doing now　　　　　26
　　　　　　　　　　　　　　　　　　　　1
What I'm doing now is important　　 31
　　　　　　　　　　　　　　　　　　　　1
It's important you know
　　　　　what I'm doing now　　　　41
　　　　　　　　　　　　　　　　　　　　1
　　　　　　　　　　　　　　　　　　 101
Look again at what I'm doing now
　　　　　　　　　　　　　　　　　　 134

Twitter™ Poem 2A

Look at what I'm thinking now.　　　 30
　　　　　　　　　　　　　　　　　　　　1
What I'm thinking now is important.　35
　　　　　　　　　　　　　　　　　　　　1
It's important you know
　　　　　what I'm thinking now.　　 45
　　　　　　　　　　　　　　　　　　　　1
　　　　　　　　　　　　　　　　　　 113
Look again at what I'm thin
　　　　　　　　　　　　　　　　　　 140

Twitter™ Poem 3   14

                                    1
Read what I write.   18
                                    1
Hear what I think.   18
                                    1
Know what I'm doing.   19
                                   73
                                    1
                                    1
Read what I write.   18
                                    1
More than I think.   18
                                    1
Next thing I'm doing   20
                                  133
                                    1
T - Off.   6

                                  140

Twitter™ Poem 3B   15

[Look at what I'm doing now!]
                                        1
Read what I say.   16
                                        1
Hear what I think.   17
                                        1
Waste your time.   16
                                        1
Tweet Off.   10
                                       77

twits *n(OED 2017 Revised)* A person who uses Twitter™.

Poem for Search Engines™
[128 bit unencrypted poem]

Poem, poem, poem, poem.
Poem, poem, poem, poem.

Poem, poem, poem, poem.
Poem, poem, poem, poem.

Poem, poem, poem, poem.
Poem, poem, poem, poem.

Poem, poem, poem, poem.
Poem, poem, poem, poem.

01110000 01101111 01100101 01101101
01110000 01101111 01100101 01101101
01110000 01101111 01100101 01101101
01110000 01101111 01100101 01101101

01110000 01101111 01100101 01101101
01110000 01101111 01100101 01101101
01110000 01101111 01100101 01101101
01110000 01101111 01100101 01101101

Last Seen on CCTV

Last grainy moments captured by chance.
On cameras in the corner
and by walls and poles that have eyes.

In the shops and on the streets
of our daily lives.

Trawled for our last images
before we could say
Goodbye.

Never alone

Never alone with a mobile phone
Less than one percent do not own.

Everyone always on-call
Never at peace, never at all.

Chattering classes, one and all
Infonoise, spreads out like a wall.

Real life connections lost to a screen.

Catching-up

Everyone's catching-up now.
Catching-up on their emails
their Facebook™ friends
their Twitter™ feeds
the TV they've missed.

Catching-up on what
while they have been offline?
Spam, posts, likes, tweets and retweets
that have passed
in the blink of an eye.

Everyone's catching-up on screens
held before their eyes.
Trying to catch-up
with a time already past
and (?now) slipping away fast.

Immersed in a Virtual Environment

From Texts to Streetview™
From Phone to Facebook™
From guide to TripAdvisor™

Living a Second Hand Life
Viewed through another's lens
        the lens of others
        the lens of another

From Postcards to Blogs
From eMails to Skype™
From Photos to Flikr™

An ever more virtual life
Perceived through the layers of others

From Reality to RealTime
From Waiting click Next
From There click Back (to Here)

Escaping a threatening modern life
With the Goggles™ of an easy and safe
Virtual Life

Engrained

Engrained in the grind
forgetting it's the good things
that keep us alive.

Concentrating on entropy
forgetting it's the heat
that warms our lives.

Worried about time
forgetting it's the moments
that make up our lives.

Disturbed by the chaos
forgetting it's the journey
that is our lives.

The Road back to Verdun

May 1970

July 2012

Verdun and The Somme

Verdun and The Somme
the two greatest horrors
mankind has ever inflicted
upon itself.

Verdun and The Somme
the closest man has descended
to creating hell on Earth
for himself.

Verdun and The Somme
and over a million men
die in the forts and trenches
by themselves.

Verdun and The Somme
and a hundred years passed
the memories are fading
despite themselves.

Verdun and The Somme
our hells to be remembered
lest we forget,
what's inside ourselves.

Verdun Now

An old battleground
   not lost to the French.
Beyond living memory
   for everyone else.

An old battlefield
   a reminder of our failing.
Something to be remembered
   the horrors we inflict
      upon ourselves.

A century passes
   and no-one actually remembers.
No-one who was there
   is here anymore.

Sur le TGV again

Sur le TGV again
returning to Verdun.
Over forty years for me
and almost a hundred
since the battle was 'won'
[perhaps tactical victory better].

A high speed journey
returning through the years
to revisit childhood memories
that illuminated the horrors of war
still undimmed in the present day.

Monument to the Victory and the Soldiers of Verdun

First night Verdun

First night Verdun
Shades of Bordeaux
Light on the Meuse
Imperial buildings glow
Then the heat fades
A dark blue sky appears
The street lights sparkle
The locals promenade
A few tourists linger
Music drifts down the Meuse
A quiet town comes to a close

Walking through the woods

Walking through the woods
from the Museum to The Ossuaire.

Walking through the silence
from the rear to the frontline.

Walking through the heat
from the dark into the light.

Walking without birdsong
from butterflies at every step.

Walking with anticipation
to the greater silence ahead.

Verdun woods 2

Walking the Verdun woods
Silent woods
Shell-shocked woods
Paths pass monuments
Silent mounds
Amidst uneven ground
Only butterfly sound
Heard all around
Silent sounds
Nothing shall pass

Men and mud

Bleeding white in the battle.
Of artillery never seen before.
Millions of shells shatter
the forests of Verdun.

And the men in the trenches and forts.
Where hundreds of thousands die.
Blown to pieces by the bombardment
reigning down from the sky.

At the Ossuaire

At the Ossuaire the workmen toil
Erecting scaffolding all around
Preparing to clean years of grime
The cemeteries (too) cleansed above ground
Markers removed, crosses abound
Neat stacks mostly of markers lying on the ground
As the grass and flowers re-laid all around
Nothing disturbs the men below ground
Preparations made for century round
As no-one left remains above ground

L.Ossuaire de Douaumont

Between their time and the future

A strange Ossuaire
Half bright and clean
Half dark dirty and old
A strange cemetery
Half old and tired
Half missing in renovation
A strange monument
Between the past and the present
Between yesterday and centenary
A strange vision
Between death and now
Between their time and the future

Le Tranchee des Baionnettes

Le Tranchee des Baionnettes

At the Tranchee des Baionnettes
the visitors arrive in their cars.
Park outside and walk fifty yards.
To a concrete rectangular blockhouse
shading those still inside from the sun.

Surprised by the lack of bayonets
they walk round it and are done.
Five minutes later back in the cars.
Leaving those forever entombed
alone in the ground.

A Centenary approaches

A centenary approaches
and the graves need cleaned.
One hundred and thirty thousand
men in the ground
know nothing of this
resting so sound.

The crosses are stacked
in piles at the side
while the grass is re-laid
and new flowers are found.
What do they care
the men in the ground.

Monument to the children
and motto of Verdun *'You shall not pass'*

They shall not pass

They shall not pass
Not now, here or evermore
Five soldiers in stone
A line never before
And then comes Maginot
La Defense never rests
Until La Patrie has passed
Old enemies become allies
And we forget the past

Inside the Ossuaire an orange light pervades.
All silent in awe of the sacrifice they made.
Every stone inscribed with a life lost.
Their bones beneath our feet
slowly turning to dust.

Fourth Stage Navigation

folding space and time
travelling through space and time
bringing back the space as time

AR: Augmented Reality

Overlays of information and connections
Overlays of people and voices.

Overlays of intelligence and adverts
Overlays of obscurity and cul-de-sacs.

Overlays of obvious and outlandish
Overlays of choice? and desire.

Overlays of decisions and dilemmas
Overlays of choice and chaos.

The Armies of Memory, and their Commander

An array of memories waiting for upload.
Waiting for programmes in machine code.

The armies of the network, and their controller.
A web of connections, waiting for data.
Waiting for commands and consequences.

Backing-Up

Backing-Up
Backing-Up into a wall
Backing-Up into a stall
Backing-Up into a fall

Backing-Up into a commentary
Backing-Up into a story
Backing-Up into a memory

Modern times make man insecure
In a way no times have done before

Degrading information storage
Drawing the line
Drawing and redrawing the data
Information storage degrading

Information Degrades

A Darwinian Dead End
[The Immortality Conundrum]

Our genes are what make us.
But if the stem cells of our children
stolen from them
could give us immortality
and so no more children
need ever be born
and we lived on forever
this would be
our Darwinian dead end.

Haunted by Malthus

Malthus returns to haunt us
Carrying capacity exceeded
When unknown to us
Sustainable solutions recede
Imminent rebound taunts us
Die-back set to proceed

Tidemarks

The tidemarks of dust
reach us every year
in our library of memories.

Washing back the past
a little less each year
our history turns to stories.

Out of time

Out of time all exits come
Every road runs out of time.

Out of time all ends are seen
Every path will reach an end.

Out of time we see the signs
Every moment is our now.

Colonia del Sacramento, Uruguay

Cephalonia, Greece

Botanical Gardens, Sydney

Looking for Zen Thrills

Not bungee-jumping
base jumping or any other
adrenalin based ing.
Mere primeval thrills
hardwired to the hindbrain.

Looking for frontal thrills
when calm appears from chaos.
From that still moment
Nature steps centre stage.
The Age of Reason proceeds.

'Lily' Leonardo da Vinci *c1480*

A New Dragon Year

An orchestra of ships and sirens
announce the New Year's arrival.

A dragon year starts and lies ahead of us.
Uncertain times, important times,
thrilling times.

A year of new dragons never seen before.
Chaotic times, momentous times,
changing times.

Doors closed, unknown till now
Doors open, unseen till now.

Chinese New Year, Singapore (2018)

Saving this spot

Saving this spot for myself
the grave-digger said
with a hint of a glint in his eye.

The best plot left I think
the grave-digger said
with a sigh and a glance of his eye.

You could book your plot now
the grave-digger said
with a smile and a twinkle in his eye.

That's a good idea I thought
think ahead the grave-digger said
with a knowing look visible in his eye.

The End of the Olympics

The End of the Olympics is in sight
when an athlete with artificial legs
competes alongside those with human legs.

The End of the Olympics is in sight
when one athlete with artificial legs
is faster than most with human legs.

The End of the Olympics is in sight
when all the athletes have artificial legs
and are all faster than those with human legs.

The End of the Olympics is in sight
when all the athletes have Nike or Adidas legs.
Then the competition is over
for those on human legs.

The Good Old Days

In the good old days
In the days of Empire and Raj
We were all just graveyard fodder
For those who ruled over us
And lived on the back
Of the toil of all our days
In those good old days.

6th Batallion Queens Own Cameron Highlanders, Battle of Loos, 26th September 1915 Joseph Gray © The Highlanders' Museum

Order and Disorder

Words
are life-support capsules for information.
Living forever now outside the mind.

Four thousand years later
first Morse then punched cards.
Then Turing machines
turned information
and everything into bits.

    Erasing information
        uses energy
            increasing entropy.

    [Landaur Limit –
        minimum energy needed
            to delete information]

Distractions

Distractions
Buzzing insects in the brain
Distractions
Pestering thoughts of possible pain
Distractions
Nagging deeds needing done now
Distractions
Annoying actions waiting in the wings
Distractions
Tiresome chores calling their turn
Distractions
Relentless routines daily return
Distractions
Always, always demanding attention
Distractions
Do I have to go on?
Have you not got something better to do?

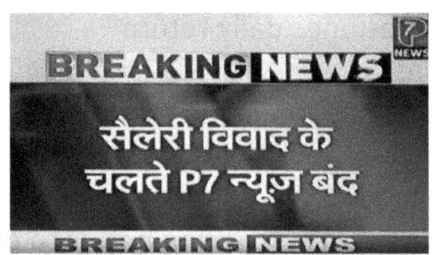

Tomorrow's news cycle

All tomorrow's papers
before I've gone to bed.

All tomorrow's news
before I've even slept.

Tomorrow's news now
breaking before you go.

Tomorrow's news cycle
won't let you go.

Among the commuters on the train

Words passing on the train.
Moments of movement and time passing.
Another day, another train, another journey.
People come and go short distances.
Every day the same train the same journey.
The time goes by but no-one notices.

Rubbish Seagulls

The seagulls appear in the Spring
drawn from the nearby beaches
to the city's open and green spaces.

The sun-lovers appear in the Spring
drawn from the nearby boxes
to the city's open and green spaces.

The rubbish appears in the Spring
dropped from the thoughtless hands
all over the city's open and green spaces.

Waiting for lunch, Sydney Opera House Café

Virtual Life Lag

Fleeting meetings in the digital age
Short contacts in your digital life
All asynchronous in the digital world
No real connection in digital time
It's never now with digital communication
We do not share a digital moment
Always behind that digital divide
Real life is now, by your side.

Dunbar's Number

Suggested cognitive limit
to the number of people
with whom one can maintain
stable social relationships –
relationships in which an individual
knows who each person is
and how each person relates
to every other person.

First proposed in the 1990s
by British anthropologist Robin Dunbar,
who found a correlation between
primate brain size and average social group size.
By using the average human brain size
he calculated that humans can comfortably
maintain only 150 stable relationships.

Dunbar explained it informally as
"the number of people
you would not feel embarrassed
about joining uninvited
if you happened to bump into them in a bar".

Adapted from © Wikipedia, May 2018

More

New Neologisms

www.NewNeologisms.com

A net to catch the web

A net to catch the World Wide Web
A World Wide Wind of data
Sometimes with eyes
Sometimes with bots.

A net to catch the bots
A World Wide Weave of connections
Sometimes with vision
Sometimes with nets

A bot to catch the web
A World Wide Wave of visitors
Sometimes with memes
Sometimes with bot nets
Sometimes with web nets

TimeJolt

Wake up the alarms have all started
the time to act has almost passed.

Wake up the alarms have all stopped
the jolt to act has passed.

www.TimeJolt.com

MindedTo

Strike when the idea is still bold.
Acting that moment before it is old.

Strike before the idea gets cold.
Acting in advance of the moment being told.

www.MindedTo.com

textexit

The penultimate one, only just begun.
Another sun, following every turn.

The ultimate one, now it must be done
                            now with added fun.
Another text, following every exit.

                                     www.textexit.com

TimeDart

A pierced moment from the past,
flies through time designed to last.

A memory arrow from the past,
strikes through reality out with our grasp.

                                       www.TimeDart.com

ChaosFix

Closing the uncertainty with a final choice.
The decision chain ends and the loop is closed.

A high plateau of certainty all choices are possible.
This is the now moment when all nexts are possible.

www.ChaosFix.com

FlatMeme

[The original point source of the growing idea.]

Moving forward through time
One heartbeat, one at a time.

One moment, each its own time
One present, always in time.

www.FlatMeme.com

ZeroDees

Travelling to the corners
of a world growing smaller.

To meet an apparent stranger
with zero degrees of separation.

> www.ZeroDees.com

EmitTime

[Create a now between two moments.]

We have entangled ourselves together
Quantum events binding us together.

A strong force holds us together
In a dark matter universe together.

> www.EmitTime.com

digitock

Digital tracks leaving so much behind
making every step harder to find.

Digital memories we have all left behind
everything remains but can't be found.

www.digitock.com

SoWhatSo

Grow up, get over it.
Move on to your new life.

So much better than the old life.
Happy to leave all that behind.

www.SoWhatSo.com

DoNoInfo

Avoiding information trails in data hungry devices, invisible steps at the machine interface.

Outside the information track
                       in memory hungry mainframes,
silent footsteps passing, without leaving a trace.

www.DoNoInfo.com

Going to Gozo

It always begins with the first line.
Hunting for that moment, out of time.

Looking for words on paper
starting afresh again.
Looking for new words on paper
something fresh again.

What I want to be, when I want.
Where I want to be, when I want.
Who I want to be, when I'm ready.

Padrão dos Descobrimentos, Monument to the Discoverers, on the Targus River at Belem near Lisbon.

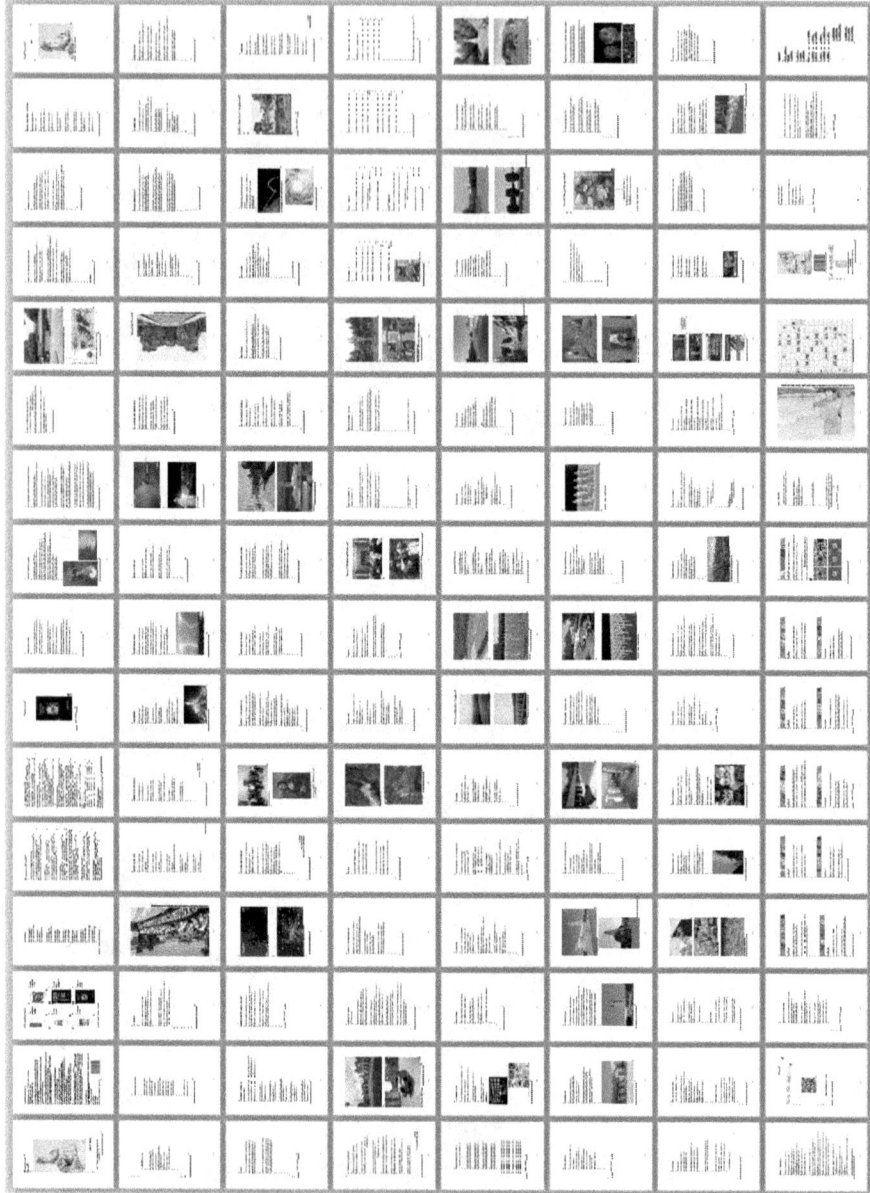

Standing at the feet of giants © Alison Boyd

ISBN 978-1-9995975-3-5

© Prohibited Publications
MMXIX
www.prohibitedpublications.com

End of the day poem
of the leftover words

When you write a few words
and give them away
they are lost forever
those words you wrote
that day.

Telendos, Greece

Jamie Inglis is a poet and doctor from Edinburgh.

Discovered Roads is his sixth collection of poetry.

He has worked and published on a wide range
of public health issues including HIV, cancer,
drugs and obesity.

He had his first poems published aged ten
and after qualifying in medicine
returned to writing poetry in the 1980's.

His poems reflect his interest in us and who we are,
the world we live in and the world we are creating.

After travelling round the world five times
he still lives in Edinburgh.

Keywords
discovered roads, Jamie Inglis, poem, poetry, travel, war, Verdun, social media, Facebook, Twitter, science fiction, Mona Lisa, neologism, timejolt, flatmeme, zerodees, digitock, donoinfo, prohibited publications, Edinburgh, Scotland

发现
的道路

警告

現在**不要**停止
別抬頭
不要再聽

不要說話　　　**不要**轉動
不要問　　　　別擔心
不要質疑　　　**不要**換

別看　　　　　　別站著
不要想像　　　**不要**採取行動
不明白　　　　　**不要**動

不覺得　　　　　**不要**這樣做
不要懷疑　　　**不要**那樣做
不要拒絕　　　**不要**做任何事情

　　　　　　　　不要做任何事
　　　　　　　　現在**不要**做
　　　　　　　　現在**不要**停止

www.ingramcontent.com/pod-product-compliance
Lightning Source LLC
Chambersburg PA
CBHW061951070426
42450CB00007BA/1236